THE BLACK KEYS
ATTACK & RELEASE

Contents

This book was approved by the Black Keys

Transcribed by Jeff Jacobson and Paul Pappas

Cherry Lane Music Company
Director of Publications/Project Editor: Mark Phillips
Project Coordinator: Rebecca Skidmore

ISBN 978-1-60378-166-4

Visit our website at www.cherrylaneprint.com

THE BLACK KEYS

The Akron, Ohio-based duo the Black Keys is well known for its concentrated, hermetic approach to recording, hunkering down with rudimentary equipment in an unfinished basement or commandeering the floor of a vacant local rubber factory to create terse but soulful rock that seems to have time-traveled into the pair's amps from some long-ago radio show. But guitarist/vocalist Dan Auerbach and drummer Patrick Carney now admit they were ready for a change of scene—as well as some company. So when they got the opportunity to work with Grammy-nominated producer/musician/provocateur Danger Mouse, a/k/a Brian Burton (Gnarls Barkley, Gorillaz, *The Grey Album*), they agreed, for the first time, to leave their familiar environs. They weren't quite willing to cross state lines yet, though.

The Black Keys had originally been approached by Danger Mouse to write songs for an album he was developing with Grammy-winning R&B legend Ike Turner, who, in recent years, had been recognized more for his contribution to the birth of rock & roll than for the time he'd spent in the tabloids. That project would never be completed, however, and the 76-year-old Turner passed away unexpectedly in December 2007.

As the pair were composing and sending tracks out to Danger Mouse in Los Angeles, ostensibly for Ike, they realized they were also instinctively laying the groundwork for a new album of their own. So when Patrick went to L.A. to visit his wife's family, he called up Danger Mouse to go out for drinks and, he says, "I asked him straight up if he wanted to produce our record. He said yeah, and we made a plan. Nothing was set in stone until about a week before we went in to record. I think Dan and I were intrigued to work with somebody as a producer because we both realized we couldn't teach ourselves anything more, and it was best to start learning from other people. When we were, like, 22, we didn't have the money to do this; by the time we were 24, maybe we thought we knew more than we actually did. Now, at 27, we maybe just realized we had stopped being broke, and stopped being dipshits, and we could learn from other people who make records."

"After doing four albums in the basement, we were ready to go somewhere else," Dan confesses, "but it couldn't just

be anywhere. Brian suggested L.A., but we said no way. We still wanted to do it in Ohio. There's this guy named Paul Hamann, who has a studio outside Cleveland called Suma. I'd done a bunch of projects with him before, band that I've recorded on the side. He's done some mastering and cut some vinyl for me. In fact, he's got one of the only studios in the world where they still cut their own vinyl. So we said we wanted to go there, and Brian said, 'Whatever you guys want.'"

The legacy, the hand-built recording console, and the engineering skills of Hamann were undoubtedly attractive to the Black Keys, but perhaps it was the ambience of the place that really sealed the deal. As Patrick explains, with genuine affection, "The place is covered with dust, it smells like a moldy cabin, and it looks like a haunted house. It was fitting for our first time of going into a real studio—basically being in a haunted house that hasn't been updated since 1973." Dan continues, "A big part of the sound of this record is the studio and having somebody like Paul, who is an old pro, recording us and helping us get the right sound. Having him there meant that we were free to jump on any instruments we wanted to add stuff. If I wanted to play organ, I could jump on it and just record it; if I wanted to jump on the guitar, I could do it. Brian and Pat had a Moog part they thought would be cool on a song, so they would just try it. That studio is a really special place."

Danger Mouse fit right in, too. Says Dan, "He came in as our collaborator. Brian does hip-hop, but he likes rock & roll, obscure '60s psychedelic stuff, and we listen to a lot of that too. So he was pretty easy to get along with. Brian has a real ear for melody and arrangement, and that was a big part of this record—his making suggestions about the arrangements."

Dan and Patrick were childhood buddies who grew up in the same Akron neighborhood and attended the same schools. But they didn't recognize their natural musical affinity until well into high school when they started jamming together with other aspiring musician friends, who they soon ditched. Early demos of the Black Keys featured a third member, who played a Moog bass, but he didn't last long either, and they subsequently carried on as a duo. Says Dan, "Pat and I just click. We walk into a groove quite easily. It's kind of hard to describe." Their minimalist approach to rock is similar to what the late-'70s New York City duo Suicide's has been to electronic dance music—the Black Keys have been able to make something ferociously noisy, deceptively melodic, and surprisingly sincere out of the simplest tools and riffs. (Unlike Suicide, though, they're more congenial than confrontational with their audiences.)

With Danger Mouse, the Black Keys didn't veer uncomfortably far from the elemental rock & roll territory they'd mined so effectively on previous albums, like their 2006 Nonesuch debut, *Magic Potion*, or their Fat Possum discs, *Rubber Factory* (2004) and *Thickfreakness* (2003). But they were definitely in a mood to experiment on Attack & Release. Dan explains, "We'd never let it all go before like we did for this one, where anything was game." The new tracks have a spaciousness and clarity that accentuate the soulfulness in Dan's preternaturally weathered vocals and in arrangements that oscillate between melancholy and swagger. (On side-by-side, moody vs. head-banging versions of "Remember When," they do both.) There's a subtle range of extra instrumentation (organ, piano,

synthesizer) and some very cool arrangements (like the ghostly choir that surfaces midway through "I Got Mine"). Guitarist Marc Ribot and Pat's uncle, multi-instrumentalist Ralph Carney—both veterans of Tom Waits' band—sat in for a few days of unfettered jamming. Jessica Lea Mayfield, an impressive eighteen-year-old bluegrass/country singer from Kent, Ohio, sings alongside Dan on the plaintive final cut, "Things Ain't Like They Used to Be."

Dan and Patrick did finally head west for the mix. Recalls Patrick, "We started August 9 [2007]; our last day was August 23. We went to L.A. to mix the record with Brian's engineer, Kennie Takahashi, who mixed the Gnarls record. He's a younger dude who knows his shit. He matched our rough mixes exactly—the EQ, the compression, everything. He just cleaned them up—or dirtied them up—from there.

"I'm more pleased with the sound of this record than any we've ever made," Pat concludes. "Rather than mask things in, like, a low-fi fog, we can make things sound big and fucked up at the same time."

—Michael Hill

ALL YOU EVER WANTED

Words and Music by
Dan Auerbach and Patrick Carney

Gtrs. 3 & 4: Open C tuning:
(low to high) C-G-E-G-C-E

Intro
Slowly ♩ = 64

Verse

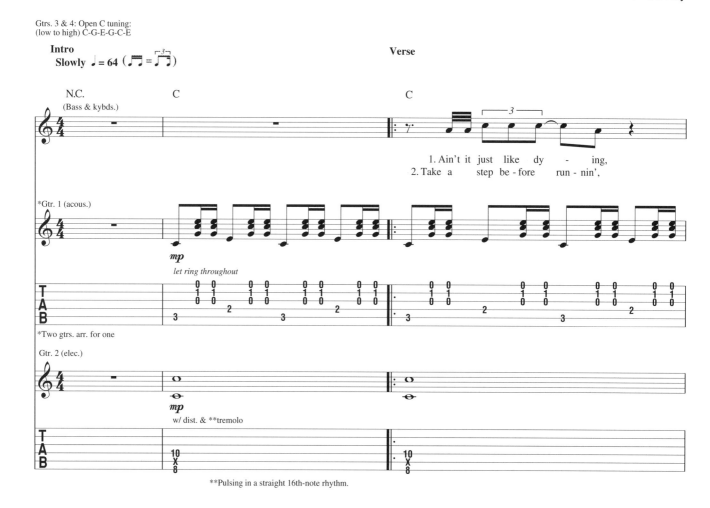

1. Ain't it just like dy - ing,
2. Take a step be - fore run - nin',

*Gtr. 1 (acous.)

mp

let ring throughout

*Two gtrs. arr. for one

Gtr. 2 (elec.)

mp

w/ dist. & **tremolo

**Pulsing in a straight 16th-note rhythm.

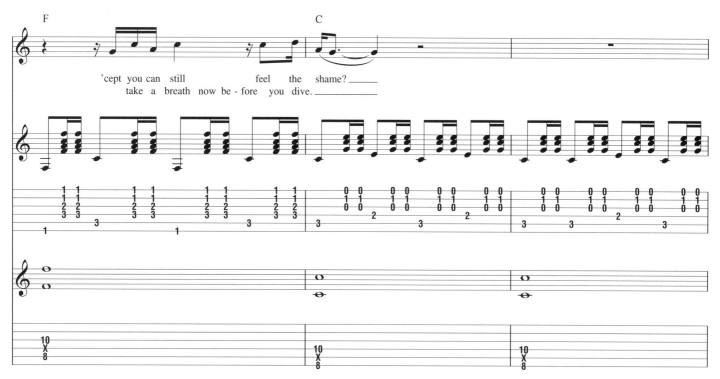

'cept you can still feel the shame? ____
take a breath now be - fore you dive. ____

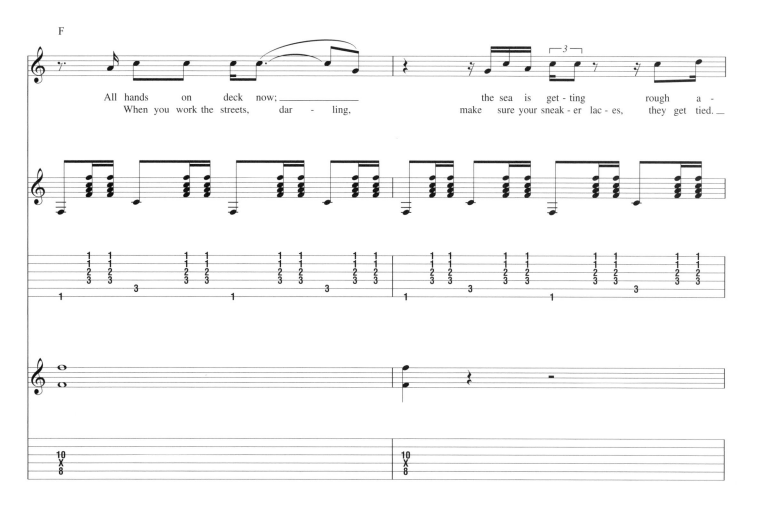

All hands on deck now;_____ the sea is get-ting rough a-
When you work the streets, dar - ling, make sure your sneak - er lac - es, they get tied. _

gain._____

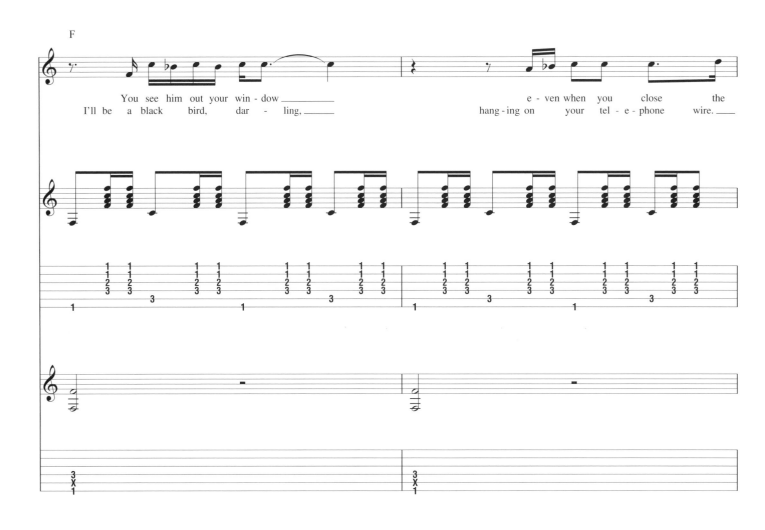

You see him out your win-dow _____ e - ven when you close the
I'll be a black bird, dar - ling, _____ hang-ing on your tel - e - phone wire. ____

blinds. _____ And all you ev - er want - ed _____
_____ Flap my wings o - ver you __

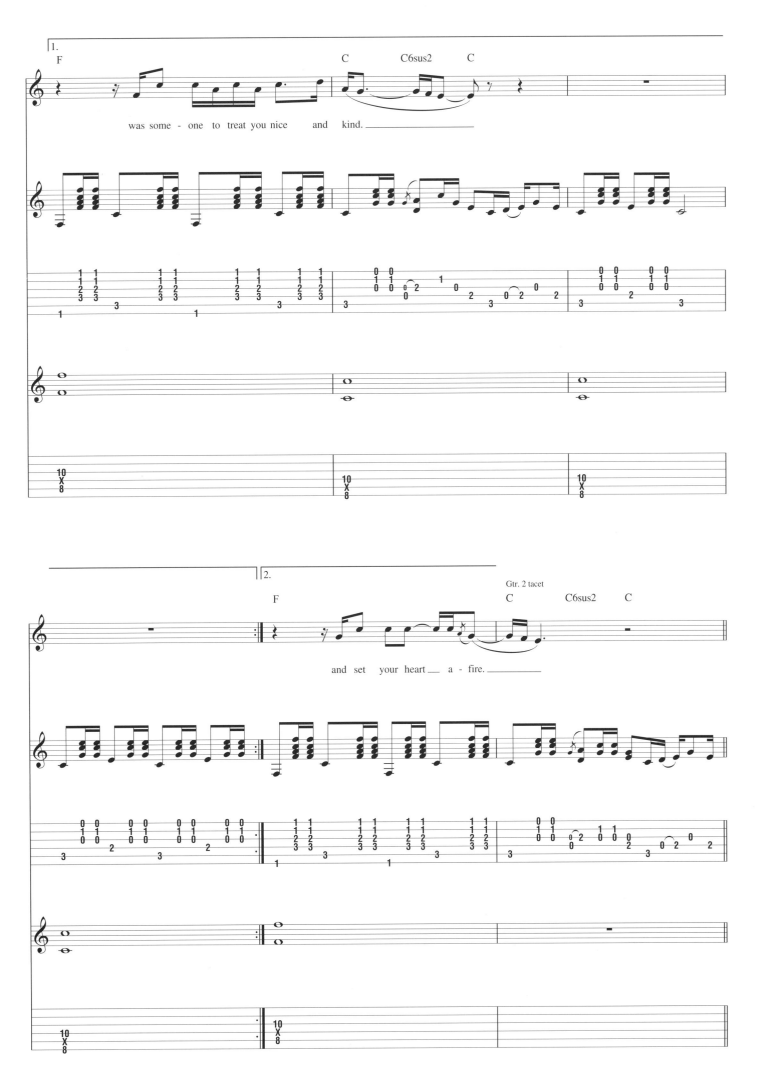

Outro

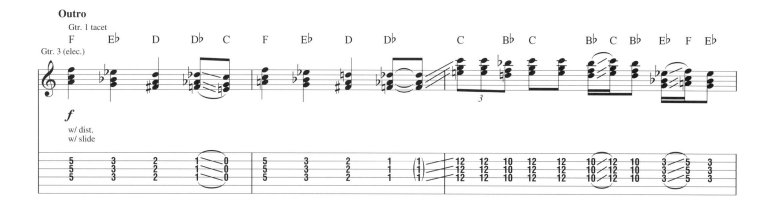

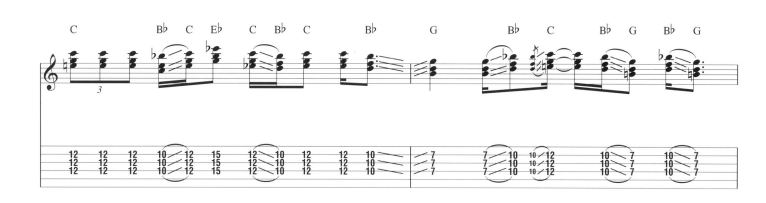

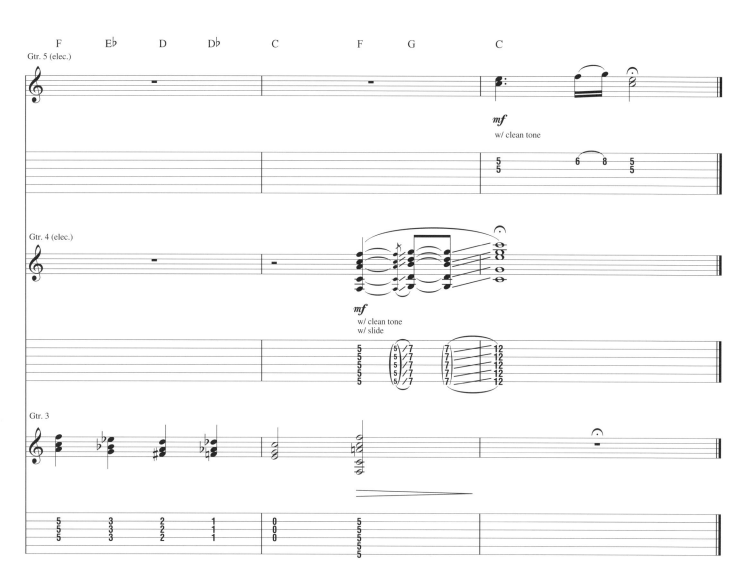

I GOT MINE

Words and Music by
Dan Auerbach and Patrick Carney

Intro
Slowly ♩ = 64

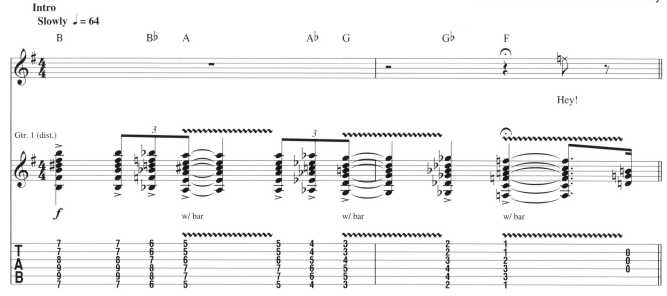

Faster ♩ = 84

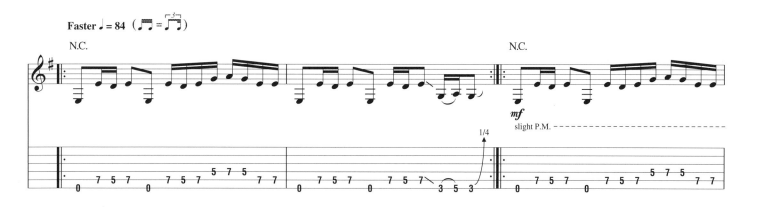

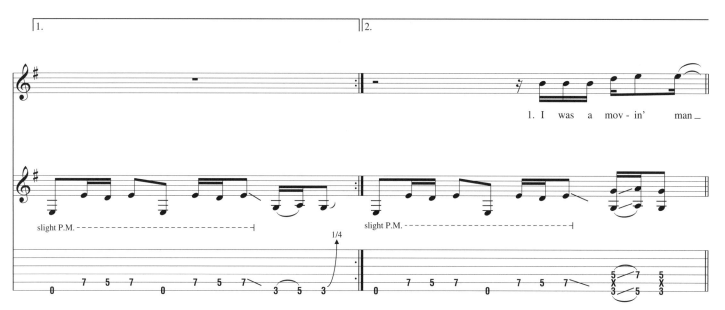

1. I was a mov - in' man

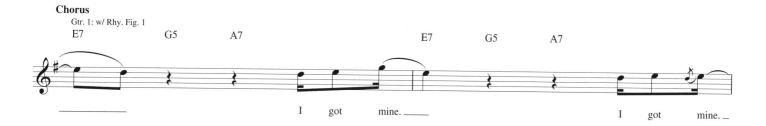

Chorus
Gtr. 1: w/ Rhy. Fig. 1

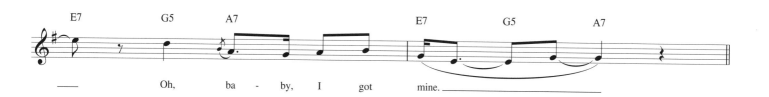

*Bkwds. gtr. arr. for gtr.   **Swell notes in with volume pedal wherever possible.

*Chord symbols reflect implied harmony (this meas.).

(Oo ___ wah, oo ___ wah, oo ___ wah, oo ___ wah.)

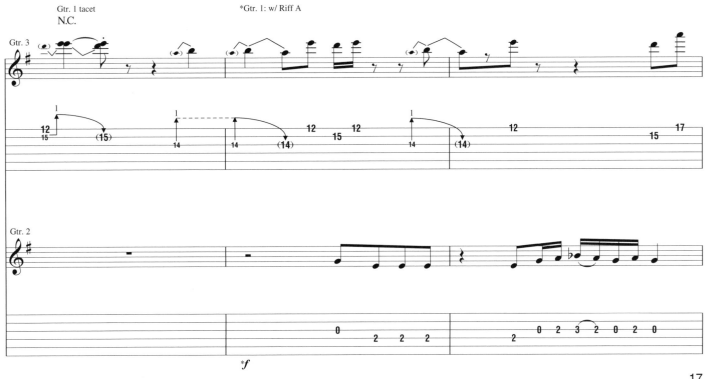

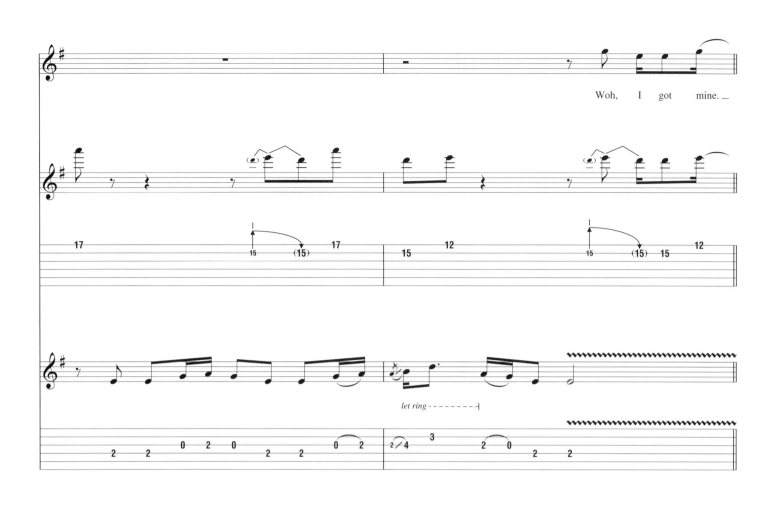

Woh, I got mine. __

let ring - - - - - - - - - ┤

Chorus

Gtr. 1: w/ Rhy. Fig. 1

| E7 | G5 | A7 | | E7 | G5 | A7 |

__ I got mine. _____ I got mine. __

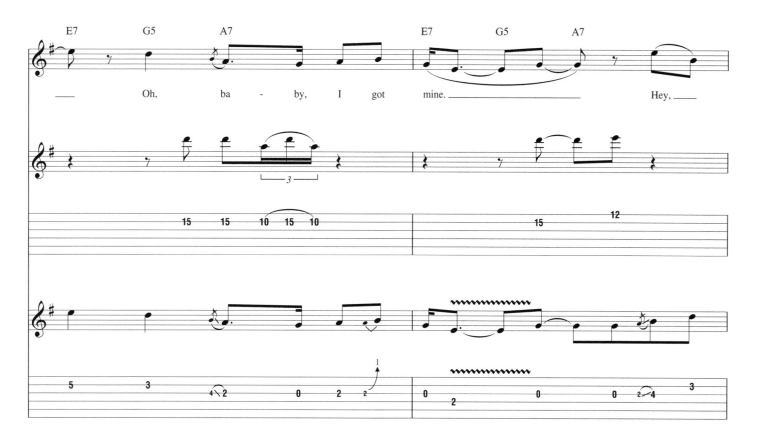

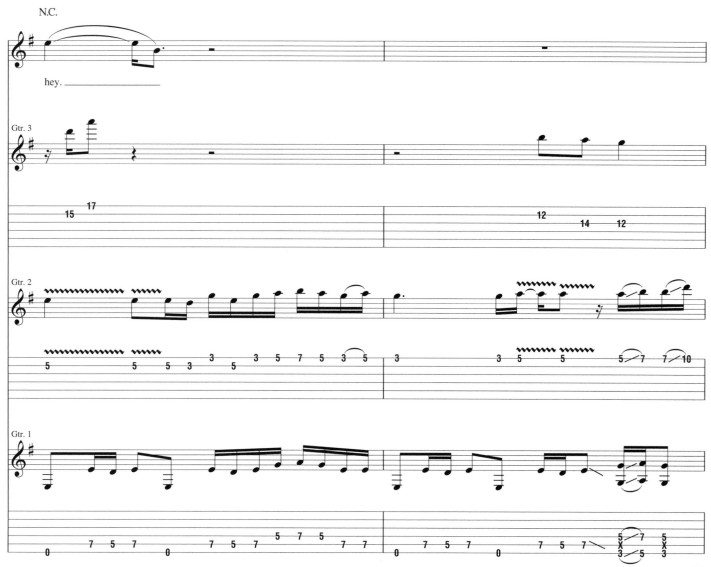

Outro
Tempo I

Gtr. 3 tacet

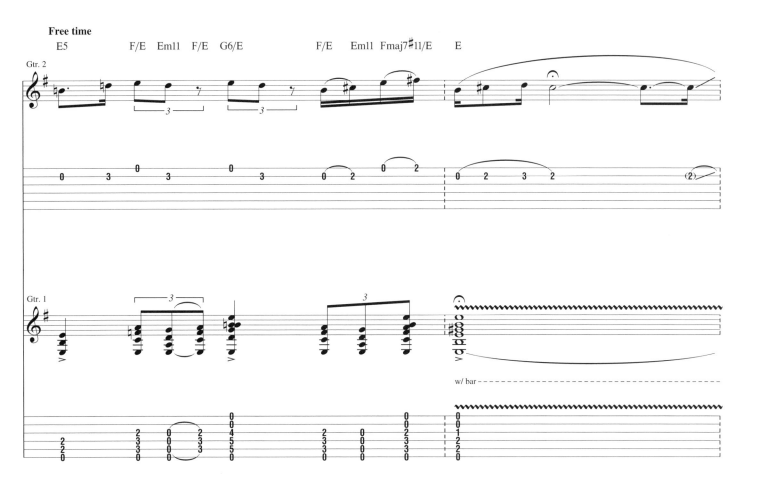

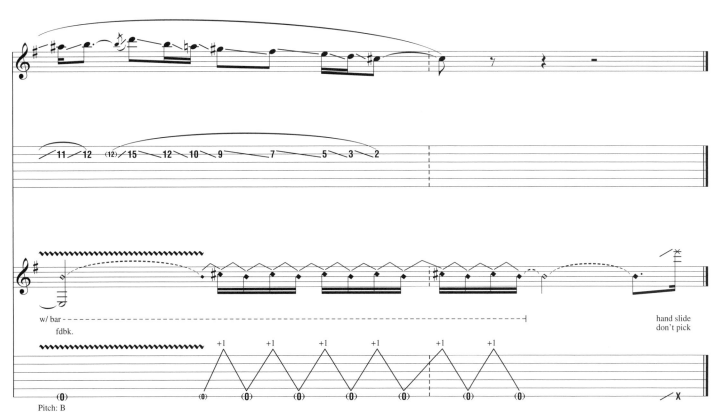

STRANGE TIMES

Words and Music by
Dan Auerbach and Patrick Carney

PSYCHOTIC GIRL

Words and Music by
Dan Auerbach and Patrick Carney

Gtr. 3: Open G tuning:
(low to high) D-G-D-G-B-D

Intro
Moderately slow ♩ = 84

*Banjo arr. for gtr.

till lat-er on _____ with no one a-round, _____ had me

fight-ing for air, _____ lay-in' on _____ the ground. _____ Oh, _____ no. _____

(Oo, _____ oo. _____ Oh, _____ no. _____ Oo, _____

Chorus

(You're) just a psy-chot-ic girl and I won't get lost _____ in your world. _____
oo.) _____ (Oo.

*Set for one octave higher.

30

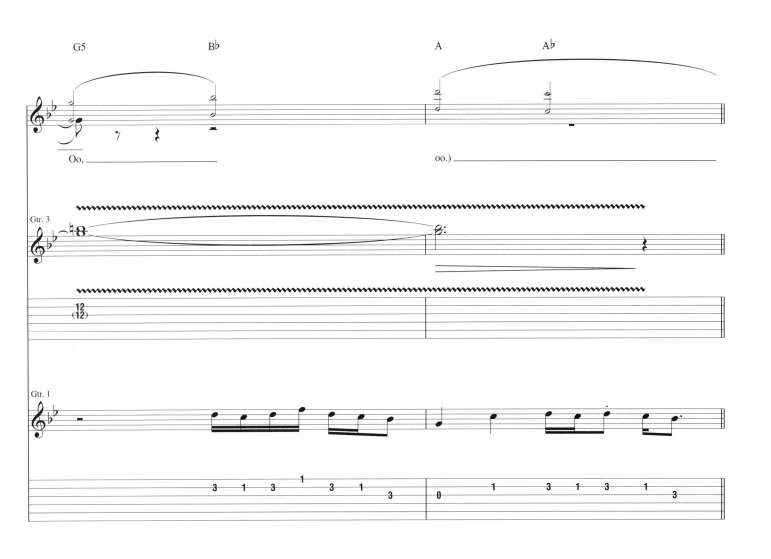

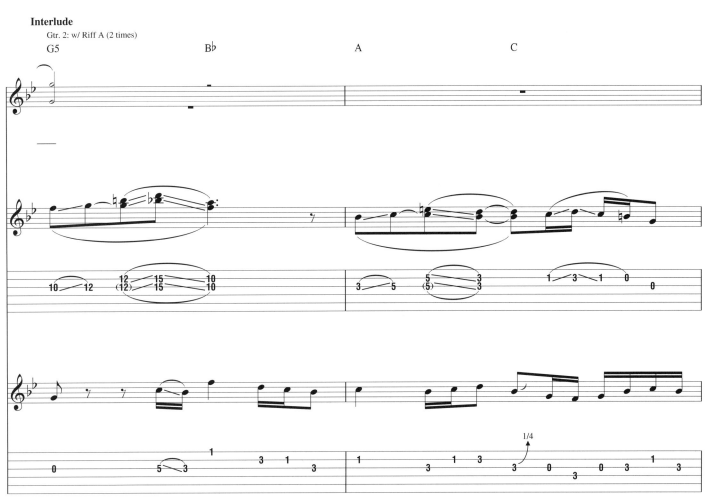

Interlude

Gtr. 2: w/ Riff A (2 times)

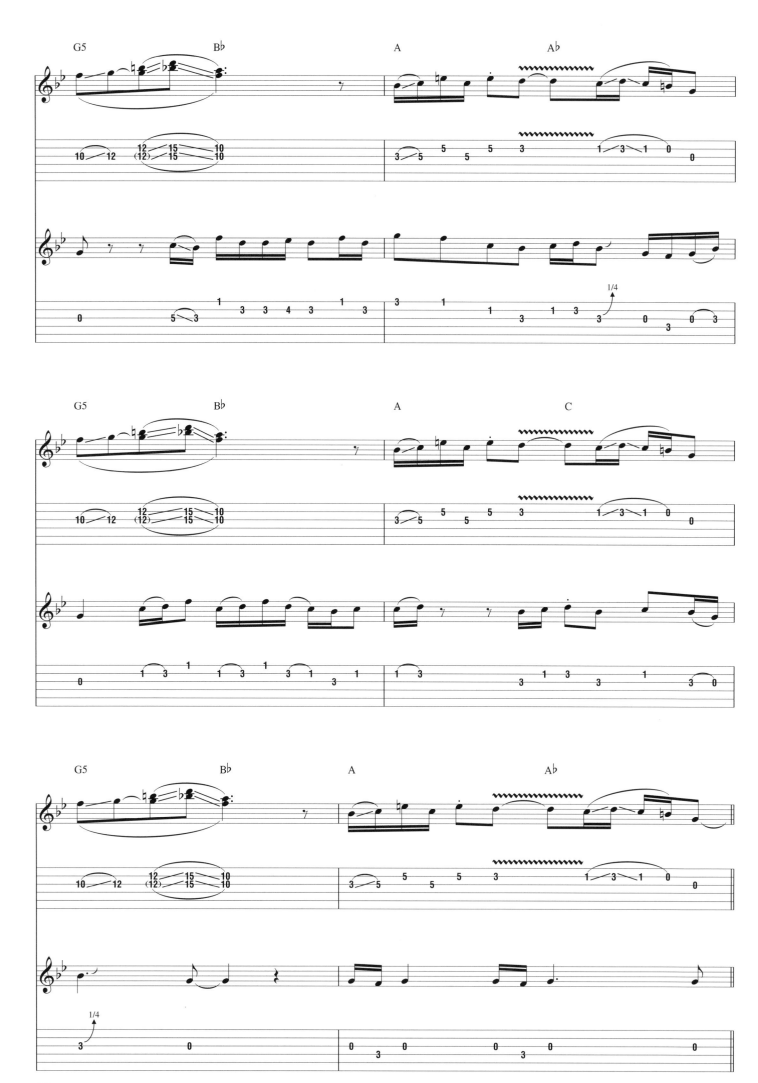

33

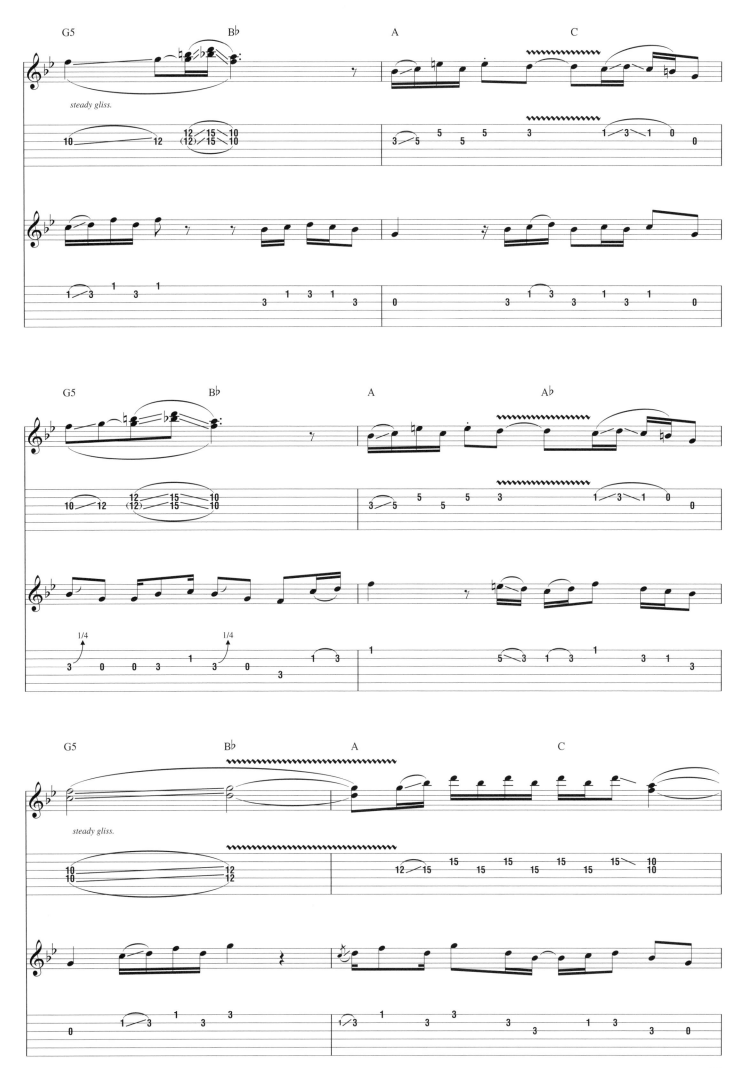

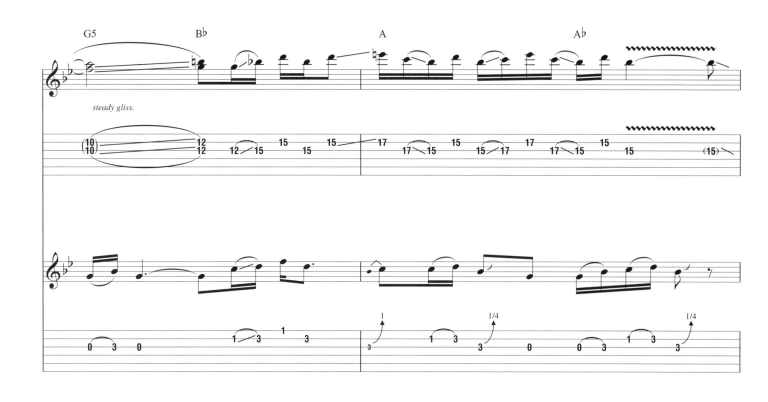

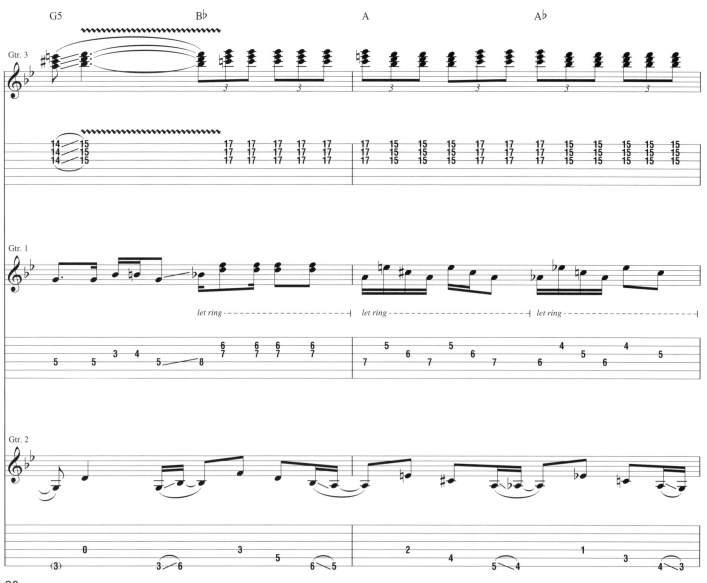

36

G5

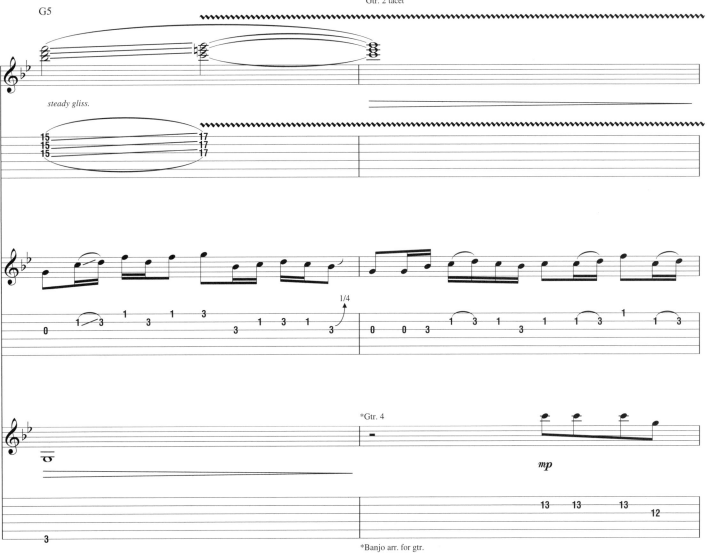

*Banjo arr. for gtr.

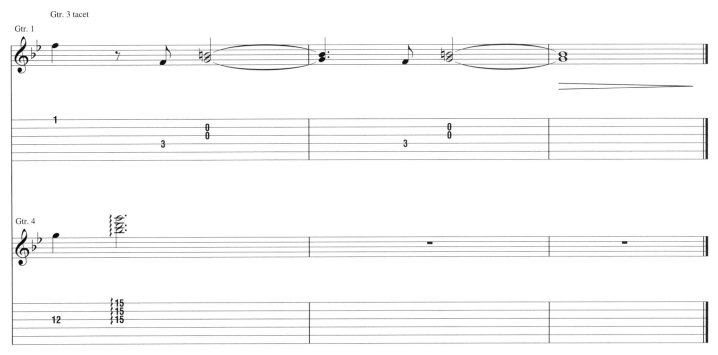

LIES

Words and Music by
Dan Auerbach and Patrick Carney

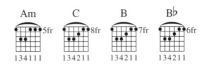

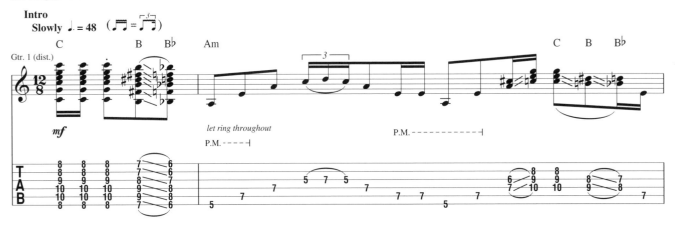

⊕ Coda

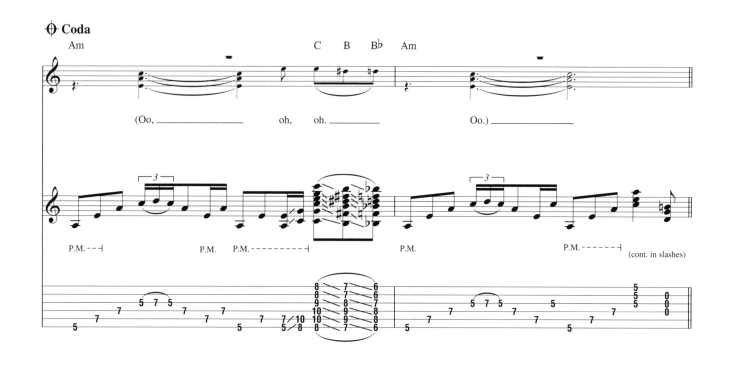

Outro

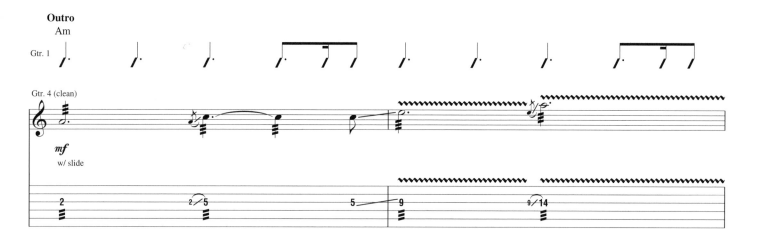

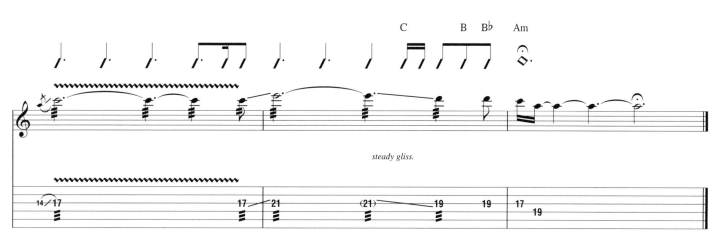

REMEMBER WHEN (SIDE A)

Gtr. 1: Capo I

Words and Music by
Dan Auerbach and Patrick Carney

Intro
Slowly ♩. = 60
N.C.

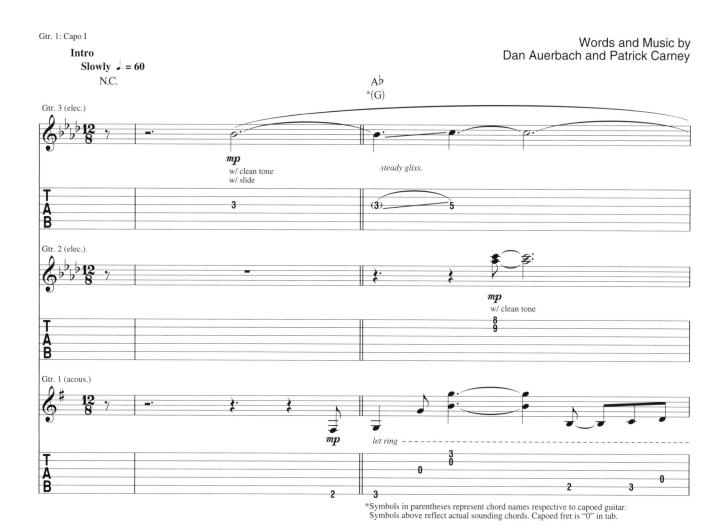

*Symbols in parentheses represent chord names respective to capoed guitar.
Symbols above reflect actual sounding chords. Capoed fret is "0" in tab.

Verse

A♭
(G)

1. It hap-pened when I _____ heard her name. __

sim.

let ring --------

let ring --------

The same old thoughts crept back a - gain, __ oh, and

let ring --------------------

let ring --------------------

45

46

smacks   you   on   your ____   cheeks _____   a - gain. ___   Oh,   it   stings, _

mm, ___   it   stings. ___

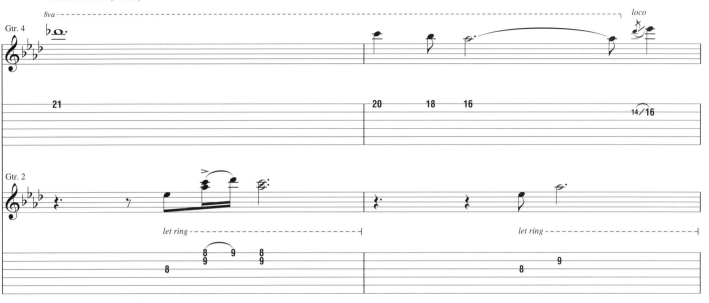

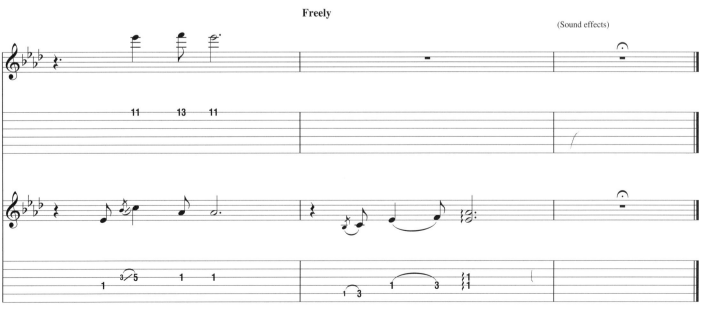

REMEMBER WHEN (SIDE B)

Words and Music by
Dan Auerbach and Patrick Carney

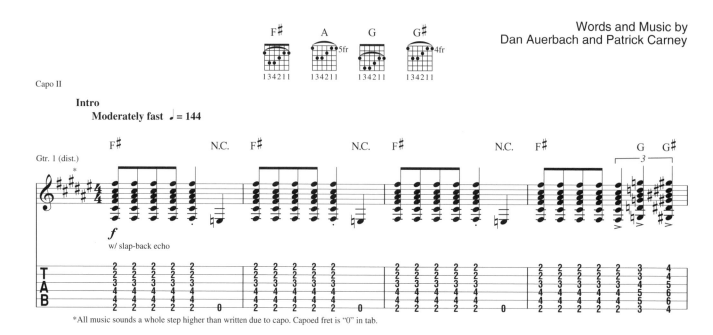

Capo II

Intro

Moderately fast ♩ = 144

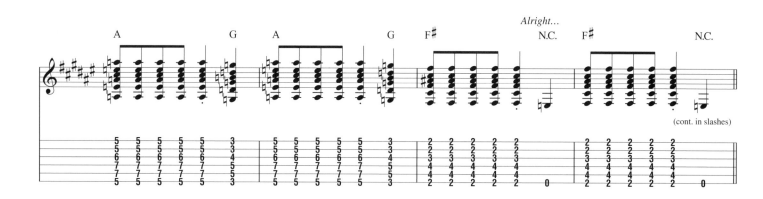

*All music sounds a whole step higher than written due to capo. Capoed fret is "0" in tab.

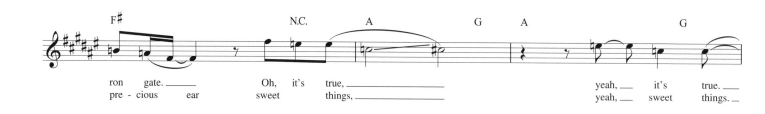

ron gate. _____ Oh, it's true, _____ yeah, ___ it's true. ___
pre - cious ear sweet things, _____ yeah, ___ sweet things. __

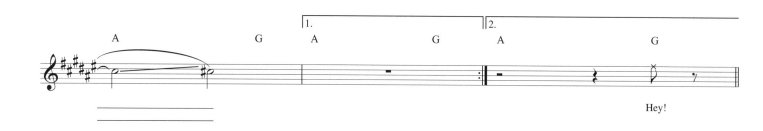

Hey!

Guitar Solo

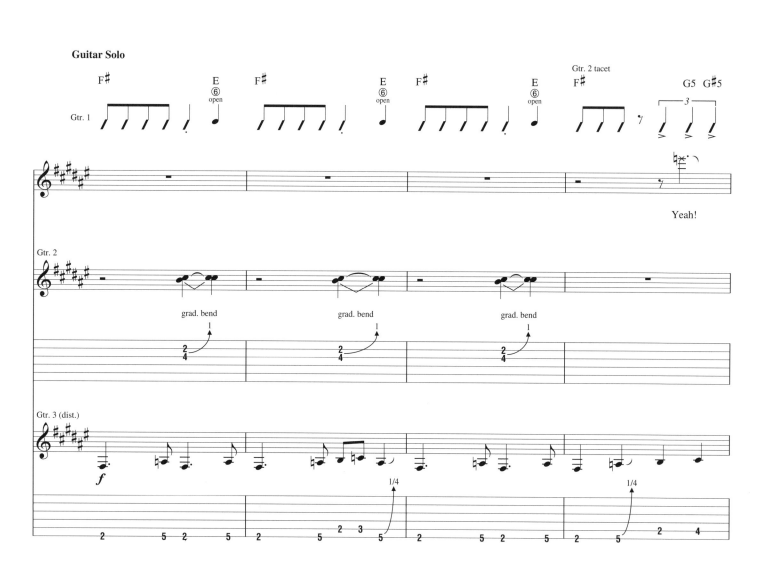

Yeah!

Gtr. 1: w/ Rhy. Fig 1 (last 4 meas., 2 times)

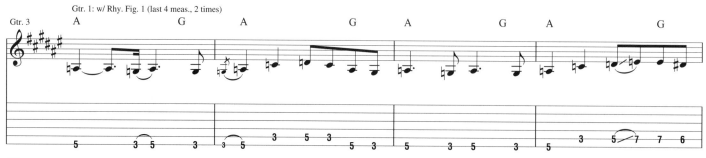

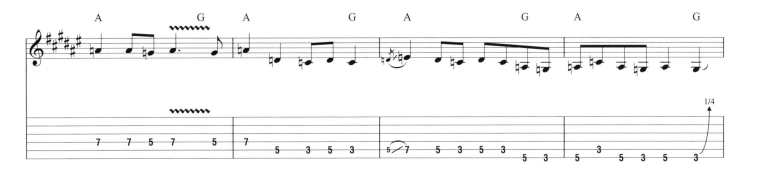

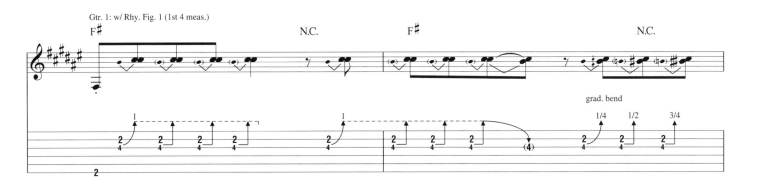

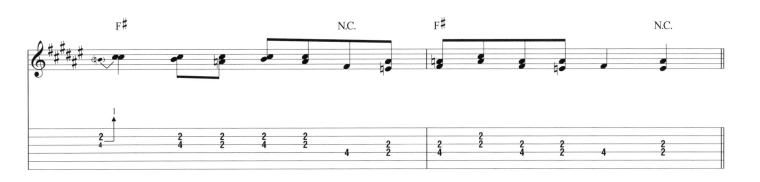

Verse

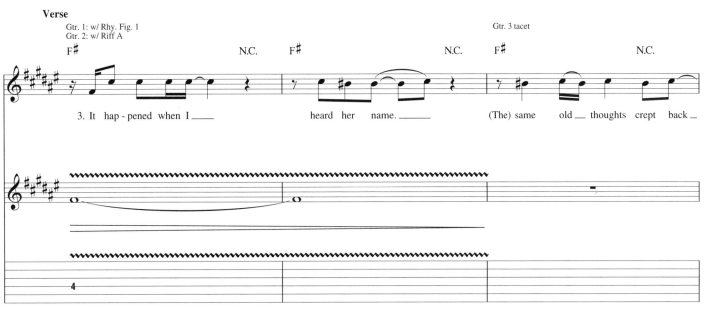

3. It hap-pened when I _____ heard her name. _____ (The) same old _____ thoughts crept back _____

a - gain,   oh, they grew,

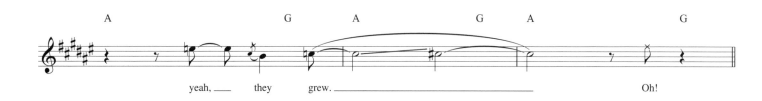

yeah,   they grew.   Oh!

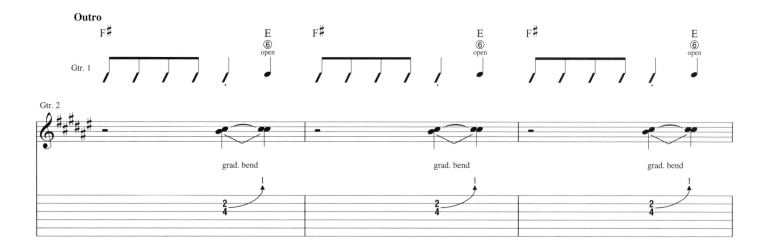

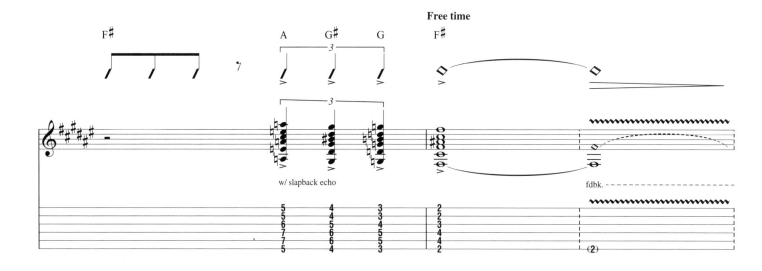

SAME OLD THING

Words and Music by
Dan Auerbach and Patrick Carney

Intro
Moderately slow ♩ = 84

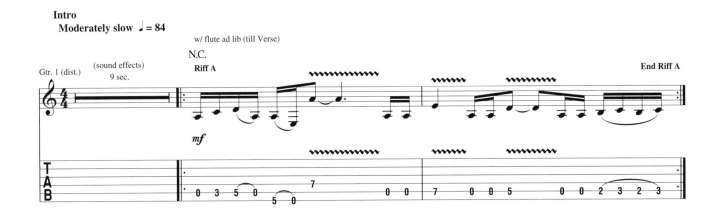

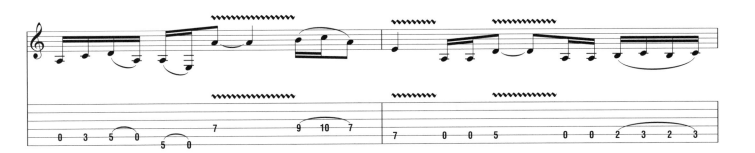

1. No mat - ter where __ you been, __
2. You got a cal - lous heart __

the peo - ple try to do you in. __
from be - ing torn __ a - part. __

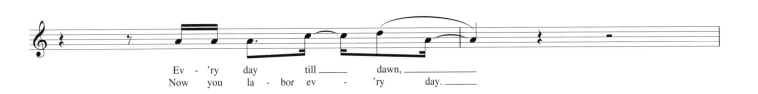

Ev - 'ry day till __ dawn, __
Now you la - bor ev - 'ry day. __

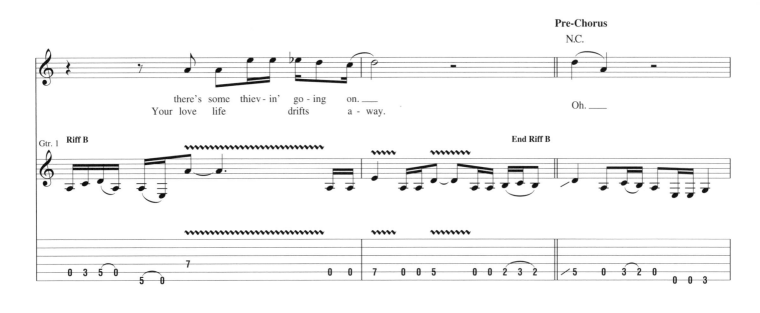

there's some thiev-in' go-ing on. ___
Your love life drifts a - way.

Oh. ___

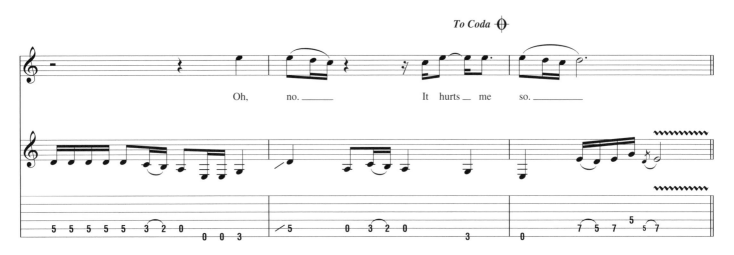

Oh, no. ___ It hurts ___ me so. ___

Chorus

Just the same ___ old thing. ___ Just the same ___ old thing. ___

___ No mat - ter how ___ much love you try to bring, ___

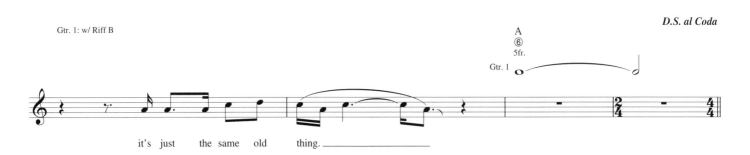

it's just the same old thing. ___

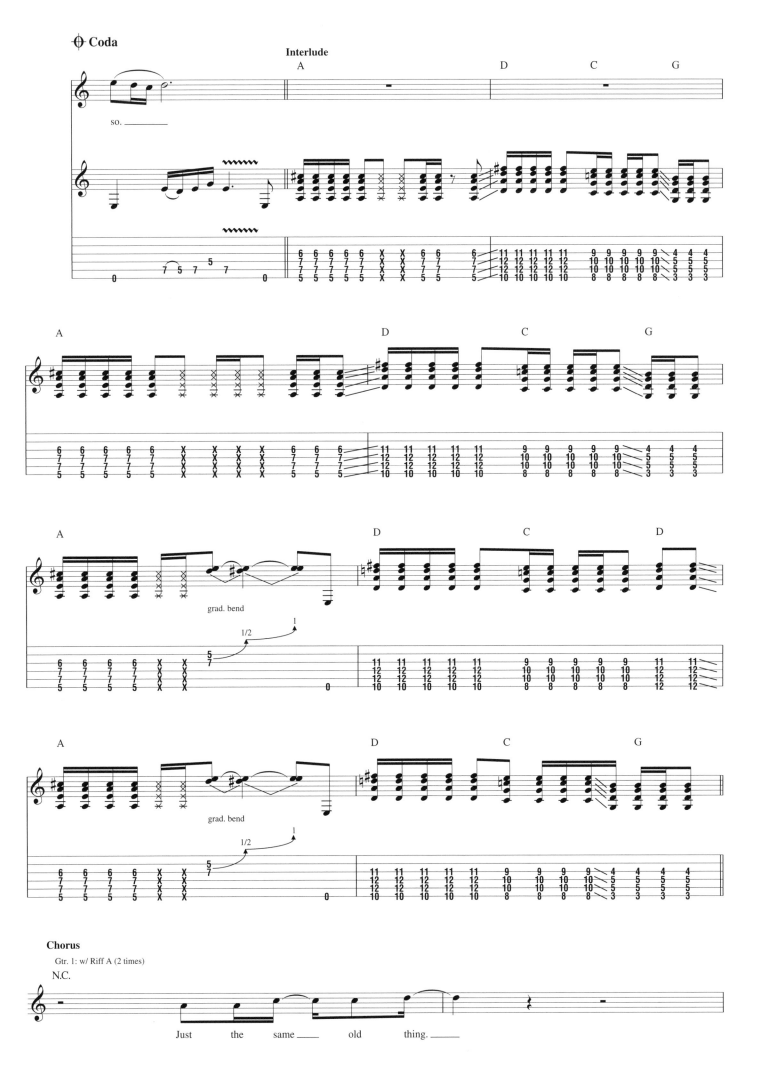

Just the same ___ old thing. _____

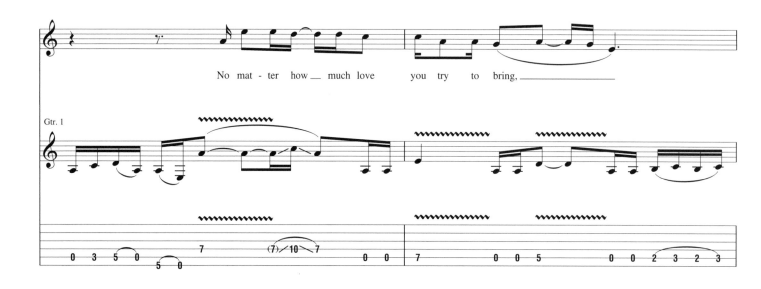

No mat - ter how ___ much love you try to bring, _____

Gtr. 1

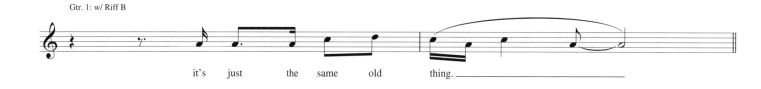

Gtr. 1: w/ Riff B

it's just the same old thing. _____

Outro
w/ flute ad lib (till end)

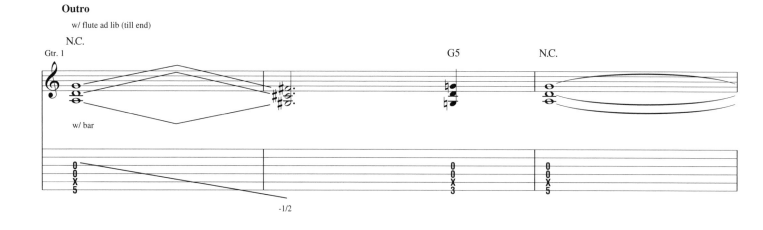

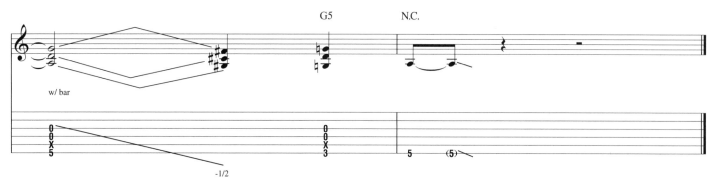

SO HE WON'T BREAK

Words and Music by
Dan Auerbach and Patrick Carney

*Two gtrs. arr. for one.

**Omit slide when recalled.

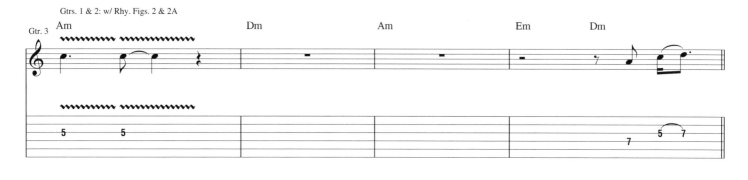

Verse

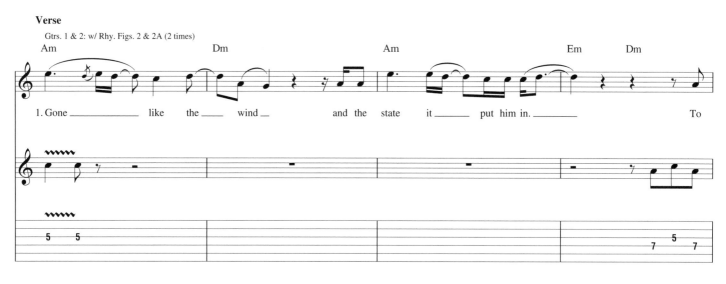

1. Gone _____ like the _____ wind _____ and the state it _____ put him in. _____ To

hold his _____ head _____ high _____ when he real - ly _____ wants _ to die. _____ And

Chorus

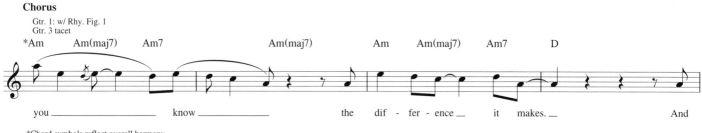

you _____ know _____ the dif - fer - ence _____ it makes. _____ And

*Chord symbols reflect overall harmony.

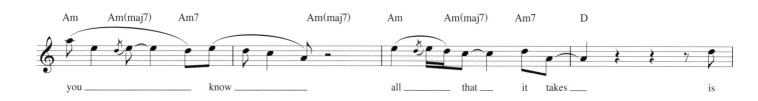

you _____ know _____ all _____ that _ it takes _____ is

Verse

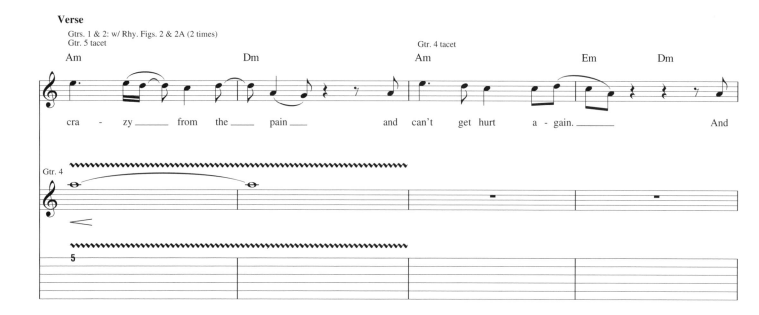

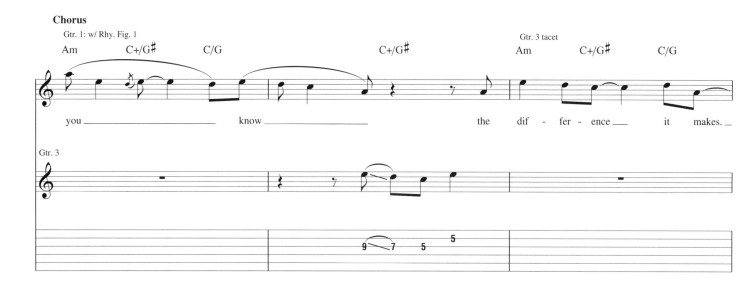

Chorus

Gtrs. 1 & 2: w/ Rhy. Figs. 2 & 2A (2 times)
Gtr. 5: w/ Riff A

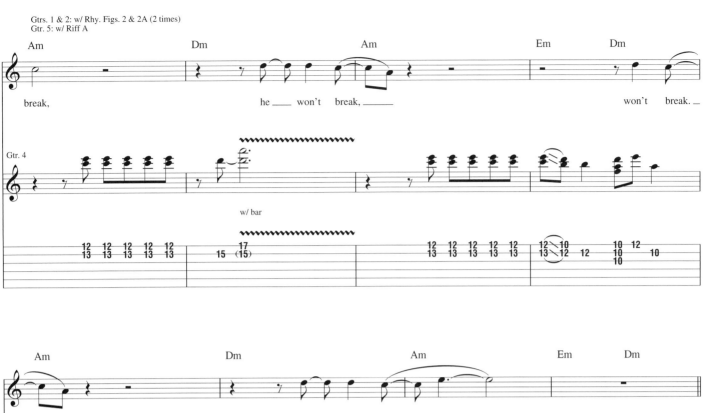

Guitar Solo

Gtrs. 1 & 2: w/ Rhy. Figs. 2 & 2A (2 times)
Gtr. 5: w/ Riff A

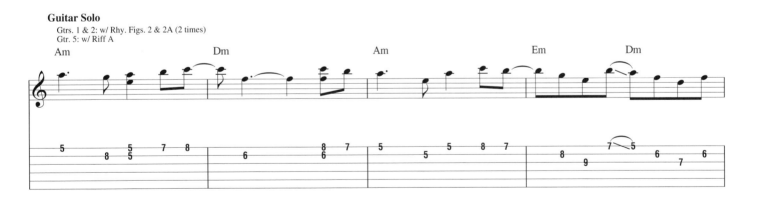

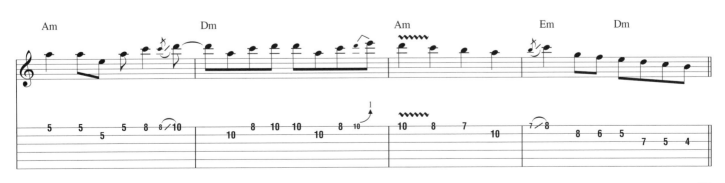

OCEANS AND STREAMS

Words and Music by
Dan Auerbach and Patrick Carney

Copyright © 2008 McMoore McLesst Publishing (BMI)
All Rights in the world excluding Australia and New Zealand Administered by Wixen Music Publishing, Inc.
All Rights in Australia and New Zealand Administered by GaGa Music
All Rights Reserved Used by Permission

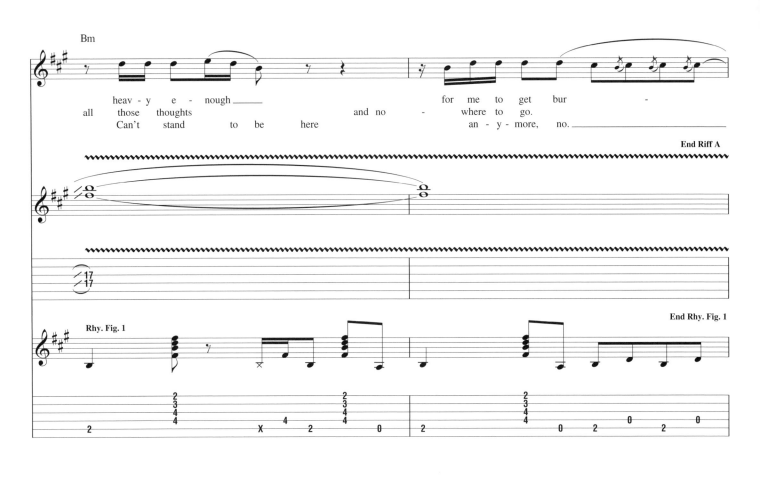

THINGS AIN'T LIKE THEY USED TO BE

Words and Music by
Dan Auerbach

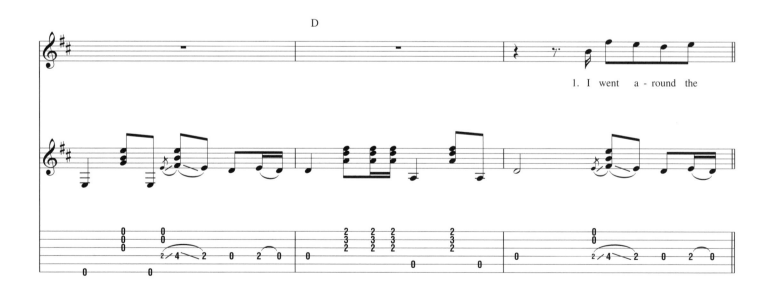

1. I went a - round the

2nd & 3rd times, Gtr. 1: w/ Rhy. Fill 2

up _____ to say... _____
good _____ on me. _____
times _____ are gone. _____

It does - n't mean a

Chorus

Gtr. 1: w/ Rhy. Fig. 1

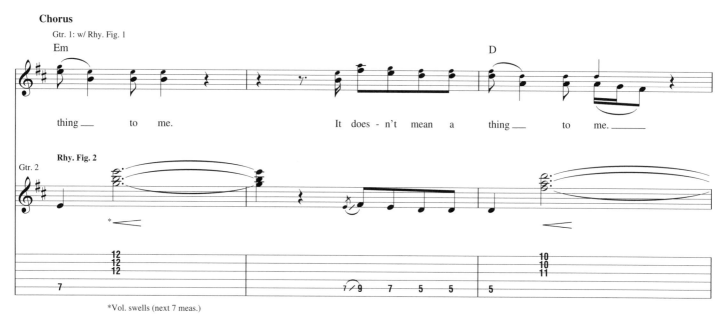

thing ___ to me.

It does - n't mean a thing ___ to me. _____

*Vol. swells (next 7 meas.)

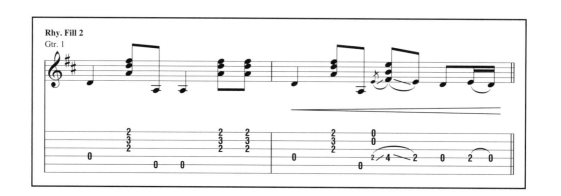

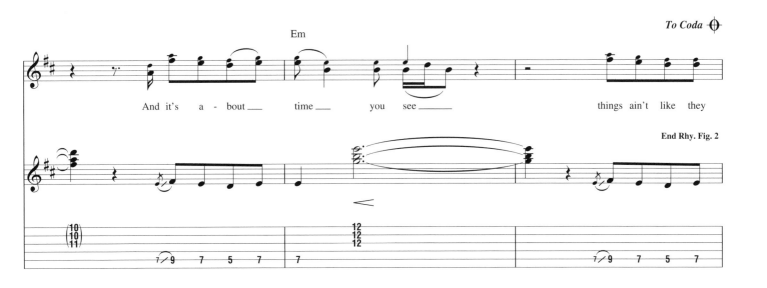

And it's a - bout ___ time ___ you see ___ things ain't like they

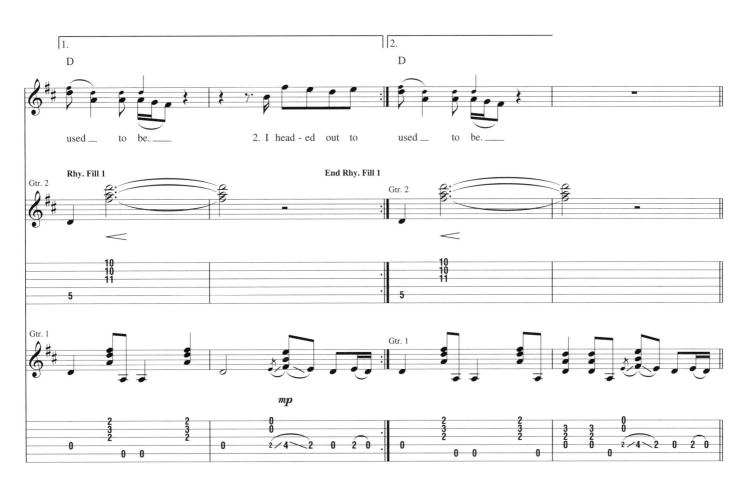

used ___ to be. ___ 2. I head - ed out to used ___ to be. ___

Guitar Solo

Gtr. 1: w/ Rhy. Fig. 1
Gtr. 2: w/ Rhy. Fig. 2

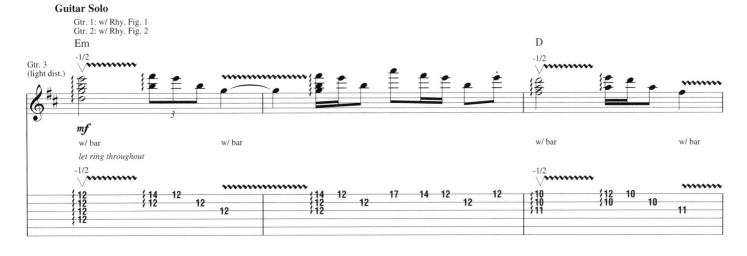

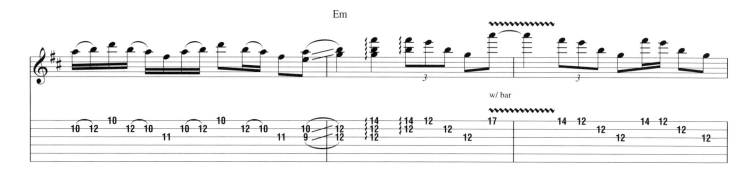

D.S. al Coda

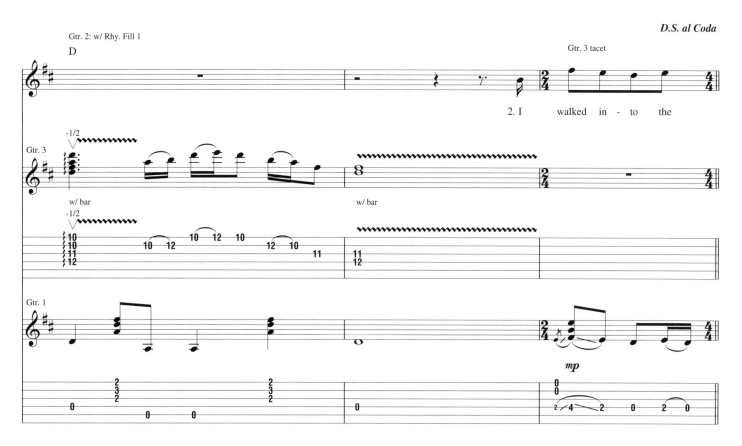

Coda

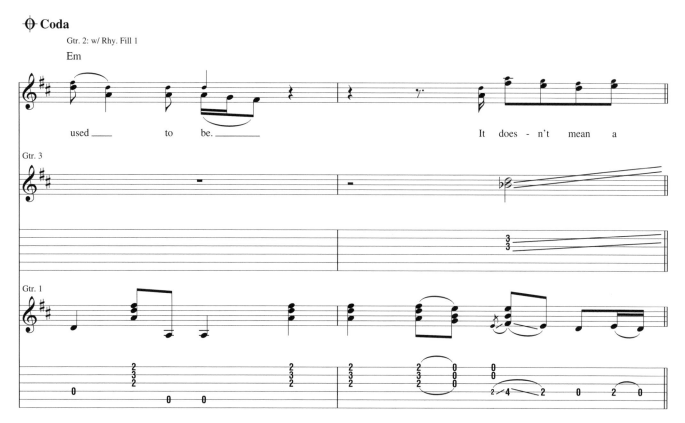

Outro-Chorus
Gtr. 1: w/ Rhy. Fig. 1
Gtr. 2: w/ Rhy. Fig. 2

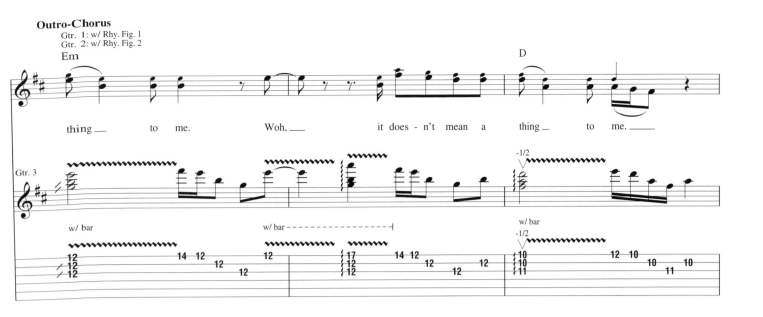

thing ___ to me. Woh, ___ it does-n't mean a thing ___ to me. ___

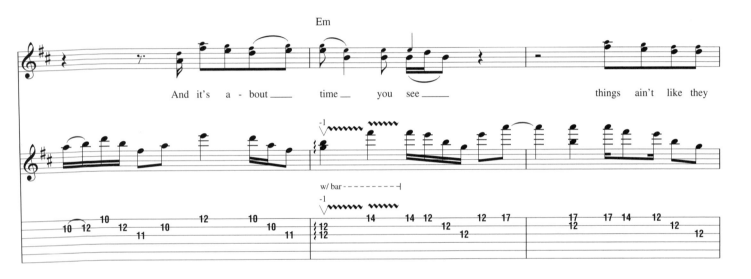

And it's a - bout ___ time ___ you see ___ things ain't like they

*Gtr. 2: w/ Rhy. Fill 1

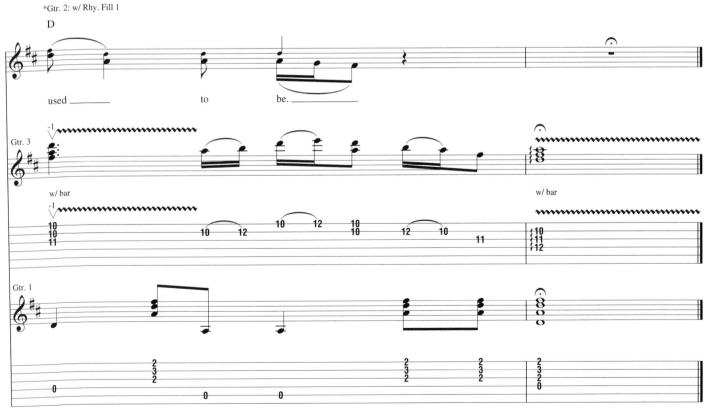

used ___ to be. ___

*Rest in last measure includes a fermata.

Guitar Notation Legend

Guitar music can be notated three different ways: on a *musical staff*, in *tablature*, and in *rhythm slashes*.

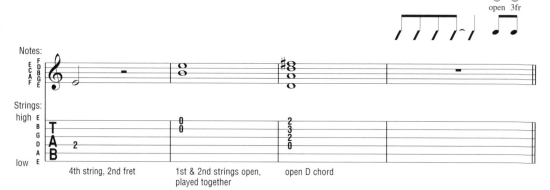

RHYTHM SLASHES are written above the staff. Strum chords in the rhythm indicated. Use the chord diagrams found at the top of the first page of the transcription for the appropriate chord voicings. Round noteheads indicate single notes.

THE MUSICAL STAFF shows pitches and rhythms and is divided by bar lines into measures. Pitches are named after the first seven letters of the alphabet.

TABLATURE graphically represents the guitar fingerboard. Each horizontal line represents a string, and each number represents a fret.

4th string, 2nd fret | 1st & 2nd strings open, played together | open D chord

---

HALF-STEP BEND: Strike the note and bend up 1/2 step.

WHOLE-STEP BEND: Strike the note and bend up one step.

GRACE NOTE BEND: Strike the note and immediately bend up as indicated.

SLIGHT (MICROTONE) BEND: Strike the note and bend up 1/4 step.

BEND AND RELEASE: Strike the note and bend up as indicated, then release back to the original note. Only the first note is struck.

PRE-BEND: Bend the note as indicated, then strike it.

VIBRATO: The string is vibrated by rapidly bending and releasing the note with the fretting hand.

WIDE VIBRATO: The pitch is varied to a greater degree by vibrating with the fretting hand.

HAMMER-ON: Strike the first (lower) note with one finger, then sound the higher note (on the same string) with another finger by fretting it without picking.

PULL-OFF: Place both fingers on the notes to be sounded. Strike the first note and without picking, pull the finger off to sound the second (lower) note.

LEGATO SLIDE: Strike the first note and then slide the same fret-hand finger up or down to the second note. The second note is not struck.

SHIFT SLIDE: Same as legato slide, except the second note is struck.

TRILL: Very rapidly alternate between the notes indicated by continuously hammering on and pulling off.

TAPPING: Hammer ("tap") the fret indicated with the pick-hand index or middle finger and pull off to the note fretted by the fret hand.

NATURAL HARMONIC: Strike the note while the fret-hand lightly touches the string directly over the fret indicated.

PINCH HARMONIC: The note is fretted normally and a harmonic is produced by adding the edge of the thumb or the tip of the index finger of the pick hand to the normal pick attack.

PICK SCRAPE: The edge of the pick is rubbed down (or up) the string, producing a scratchy sound.

MUFFLED STRINGS: A percussive sound is produced by laying the fret hand across the string(s) without depressing, and striking them with the pick hand.

PALM MUTING: The note is partially muted by the pick hand lightly touching the string(s) just before the bridge.

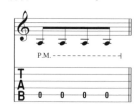

RAKE: Drag the pick across the strings indicated with a single motion.

TREMOLO PICKING: The note is picked as rapidly and continuously as possible.

VIBRATO BAR DIVE AND RETURN: The pitch of the note or chord is dropped a specified number of steps (in rhythm), then returned to the original pitch.

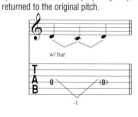

VIBRATO BAR SCOOP: Depress the bar just before striking the note, then quickly release the bar.

VIBRATO BAR DIP: Strike the note and then immediately drop a specified number of steps, then release back to the original pitch.

80